FIRST SCIENCE LIBRARY
Animals & Plants

- 10 EASY-TO-FOLLOW EXPERIMENTS FOR LEARNING FUN
- FIND OUT ABOUT NATURE AND HOW THINGS LIVE!

WENDY MADGWICK

ARMADILLO

This edition is published by Armadillo,
an imprint of Anness Publishing Ltd, 108 Great Russell Street,
London WC1B 3NA; info@anness.com

www.annesspublishing.com

If you like the images in this book and would like to investigate using them for publishing, promotions or advertising, please visit our website www.practicalpictures.com for more information.

Publisher: Joanna Lorenz
Designer: Anita Ruddell
Illustrations: Catherine Ward/Simon Girling Associates
Photographer: Andrew Sydenham
Many thanks to JD, Kondwani, Liuzayani, Poppy and Shinnosuke
    for appearing in the book
Production Controller: Wendy Lawson

PUBLISHER'S NOTE
Although the advice and information in this book are believed to be accurate and true at the time of going to press, neither the authors nor the publisher can accept any legal responsibility or liability for any errors or omissions that may have been made nor for any inaccuracies nor for any loss, harm or injury that comes about from following instructions or advice in this book.

Words that appear in **bold** in the text are explained in the glossary on page 32.

Manufacturer: Anness Publishing Ltd, 108 Great Russell Street, London WC1B 3NA, England
For Product Tracking go to: www.annesspublishing.com/tracking
                          Batch: 7005-22863-1127

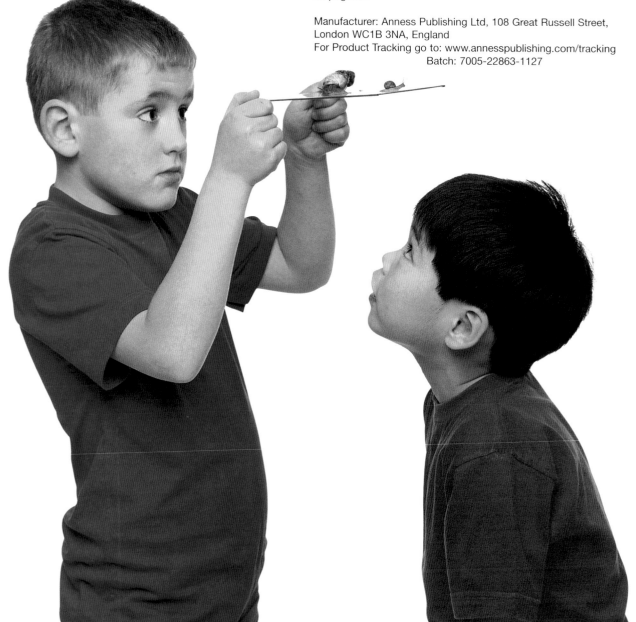

Contents

Looking at living things

Living things come in all shapes and sizes. This book looks at some plants and animals to see how they live. Here are some simple rules you should follow before doing an activity.

• Tell a grown-up what you are doing. Ask him or her if you can do the activity. You may need to ask him or her to help with some of the activities.

• Always read through the activity before you start.

• Collect all the materials you will need and put them on a tray.

• Make sure you have enough space to set up your activity.

• Be careful when you collect small animals. Do not hurt them. Do not keep them for more than two days. Always put them back where you found them.

• Watch what happens carefully.

• Keep a notebook. Draw pictures or write down what you did and what happened.

• Always clear up when you have finished. Wash your hands.

▶ This bee is attracted by the brightness and smell of the flowers. Find out how to puzzle a bee with your own flower on page 11.

What is life?

Objects in the world can be put into two groups
– living and non-living. Living things come in
all shapes and sizes, but they all take in 'food'.
This helps them grow, have babies and
respond to the world around them.

Alive or not?
Look at this picture. Which things
are alive and which are not?

The plastic brick, stone, salt,
glass, cup and straws are
not alive. The girl, dog,
plant, worms and spider
are alive. The apple
was alive before it
was picked!

Rock animals

Though rocks are not alive, they can make good toy animals. Let's make one.

You will need: small oval stones, water, small and large beads, wool, strong glue, paper, round-ended scissors, felt-tipped pens.

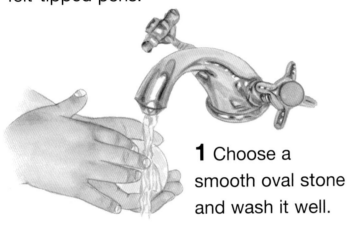

1 Choose a smooth oval stone and wash it well.

2 Glue two small beads at one end of the stone for eyes.

3 Cut out two ear shapes from paper. Glue them to the head.

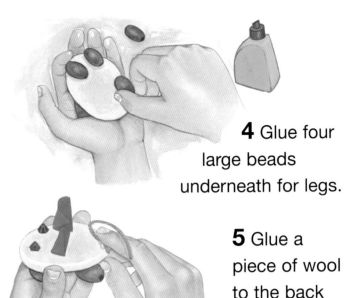

4 Glue four large beads underneath for legs.

5 Glue a piece of wool to the back of the stone for a tail.

See how many different kinds of animal you can make.

7

Going green

Plants do not eat as you do. They make their food from sunlight, water and carbon dioxide gas. This is called **photosynthesis**.

▲ Trees are plants. They cannot move around, but they are alive. Trees can live for hundreds of years.

► Ferns are plants that do not have flowers.

Plenty of plants

These plants look different but they all have the same parts. Plants have roots to anchor them in the ground. They are supported by stems and their green leaves make food. Dig up a weed and look for these parts.

Thirsty plants

If you do not water most plants they will die. Find out how much water a plant sucks up.

You will need: jar, water, clear film (plastic wrap), sharp pencil to make a hole in the clear film, plastic bag, plant with roots, felt-tipped pens, string.

1 Cover a jar of water with film. Make a hole in the film. Push a plant into the water. Mark the water level with a felt-tipped pen.

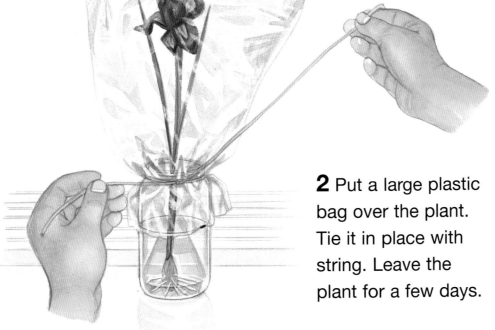

2 Put a large plastic bag over the plant. Tie it in place with string. Leave the plant for a few days.

3 The water level should be lower. You should see water drops on the inside of the plastic bag.

The water has risen up the plant stem into the leaves. **Water vapour** lost through the leaves has cooled on the plastic bag. It has formed drops of water.

Flower power

Flowers come in all shades, shapes and sizes. They contain male **pollen** cells and female **ovules** or egg cells.

▲ Bees visit flowers to drink the **nectar**. They take pollen from one flower to another. Pollen looks like a yellow powder. Sometimes pollen is spread by the wind.

Pretty flowers

Look at this lily. The pale pink parts are the **petals**. Pollen is made by the **anthers**. Pollen from other lilies is collected on the **stigma**. This is in the middle of the flower.

False flowers

Make a paper flower and see if bees will visit it.

You will need: bright tissue paper, round-ended scissors, thin wire, sticky tape, perfume.

1 Cut out a flower shape from bright tissue paper.

2 Push a piece of thin wire through the middle of the flower.

3 Squash the base of the flower together. Tape the bottom of the flower to the wire.

4 Sprinkle a drop of perfume on the flower.

Put your paper flower outside with some other flowers. Watch and see if bees visit your flower.

A bee may be fooled by your flower. Bees are attracted to flowers by the smell and appearance.

Fruits and seeds

When a male pollen cell joins with an ovule, a **seed** is formed. Seeds grow in **fruits**. Fruits can be hard like acorns or soft like tomatoes.

You will need:

apple and other fruits such as a tomato, a broad (fava) bean and an acorn. Ask an adult to cut the fruits.

◄ This is a conifer tree. It has **cones** instead of flowers. Seeds grow inside each cone.

Look at these fruits. Can you see the seeds? Cut an apple through the middle. Count the seeds inside. Draw the apple and its seeds. Collect some more fruits and look at their seeds.

Fly away

Plants cannot move around, so they spread their seeds in other ways.

You will need:
three sycamore seeds, round-ended scissors. Ask a friend to help you.

1 Collect three sycamore seeds. Leave one seed whole. Cut off one wing from a second seed. Cut off both wings from the last seed.

Which seed spins the best? Which one travels furthest? Why do sycamore seeds have wings?

The seed with both wings spins best and travels furthest. The wings on sycamore seeds help them travel away from the parent tree. Can you think of other ways in which seeds are spread?

2 Go outside with a friend on a fairly windy day. Hold the seeds at the same height. Twirl them round and let them go.

Get growing

A seed can grow into a new plant.
What does a seed need to **germinate**
and grow? Let's find out.

Cress head

You will need: four empty clean egg shells,
four egg cups, absorbent cotton, potting
compost (soil mix), water, teaspoon,
mustard cress seeds, empty food can
to cover one egg shell, pencil, paper.

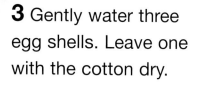

1 Put four empty egg shells in egg
cups. Fill one with compost. Fill the
other three with absorbent cotton.

2 Sprinkle some cress seeds on the top
of each one.

3 Gently water three
egg shells. Leave one
with the cotton dry.

4 Put the shells on a window sill. Put an
empty food can over one shell filled with
wet cotton. No sunlight will reach these
seeds. Check your seeds every day.
Gently water the wet ones if they feel dry.

5 Look at them after about a week. Which seeds have grown? Which seeds look green and healthy? Which seeds have grown the most? Make a chart of what you find.

The seeds without water should not have grown. Those without sunlight should look unhealthy and pale. Those grown in the sunlight should be green and healthy. The seeds grown in potting compost should have grown the most. Cress seeds need sunlight, water and food to grow well.

wet compost   wet cotton   wet cotton and no sunlight   dry cotton

No legs

Animals come in all shapes and sizes. Most animals can move, but they don't all have legs.

One foot

You will need: snail, pane of glass.

Carefully collect a snail from the garden. Put it on a pane of glass. Look at its shell. Look at its soft body and head with four **tentacles**.

Watch how the snail moves. Can you see a slimy trail? The snail moves on a big muscle called its foot. Ripples pass down the foot from front to back. These carry the snail along. The slime helps the snail move easily.

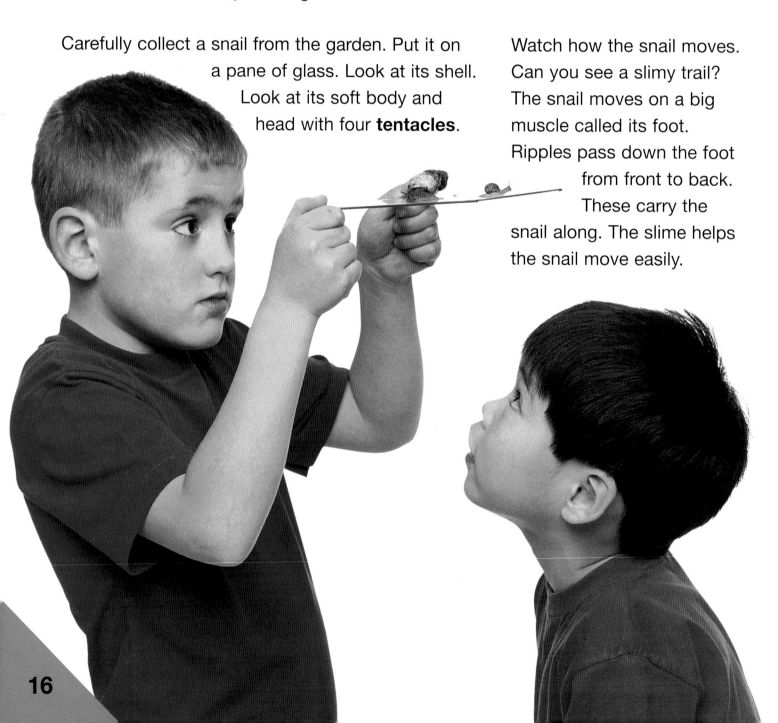

Wriggle along

You will need: wooden board or a piece of stiff paper, small trowel to collect an earthworm. You might need the help of a grown-up.

Carefully collect an earthworm from the garden. Place it on a wooden board or a piece of stiff paper. Gently feel its soft body. Watch the earthworm move. It moves by changing its shape. It grips the ground with its back end and pushes forward its front end.

▲ A squid uses a jet of water to push itself through the ocean.

It becomes long and thin. It then grips with its front end and pulls its back end forwards. The worm becomes short and fat.

Legs, legs, legs

We walk on two legs. Cats and dogs have four legs. Many other animals have more.

You will need: a small spade to help you collect creepy crawlies, small clear plastic containers, paper, pencil. For the antery you will need a large clear plastic box or jar, sandy soil (mix ordinary soil with sand to make a light sandy soil), fine net, black ants and ant eggs.

Creepy crawlies

Carefully collect some small creatures like those in the photograph. Ask a grown-up to help you. Look at the animals and draw them. Count their legs. Put the animals back where you found them afterwards.

Beetles, flies and bees are insects with six legs. Spiders have eight legs. Woodlice have 14 legs. A centipede has between 30 and 354 legs. A worm has no legs.

Active ants

You can watch how ants live by making an antery.

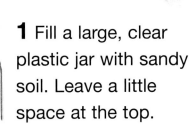

1 Fill a large, clear plastic jar with sandy soil. Leave a little space at the top.

3 Make a small hole in the soil. Put the eggs and ants in the hole. Cover the jar with fine net. Leave the ants for several days. Watch what happens.

Ants live together in a **colony**. They make a nest of tunnels in the soil. There are different kinds of ants. The queen ant lays eggs. Worker ants gather food, guard the colony and look after the queen and her eggs.

2 Carefully collect some black ants and their eggs from an ants' **nest**. Ask a grown-up to help you.

Lights out

Some animals like to live in the light. Others prefer to live in dark places.

▲ Dragonflies hunt in the day. Their huge eyes help them spot a tasty meal.

▲ Bats live in dark caves and buildings in the daytime. At night they come out to feed.

Dark or light?

1 Put a layer of damp soil in three large, clear plastic boxes. Collect some woodlice, spiders and centipedes.

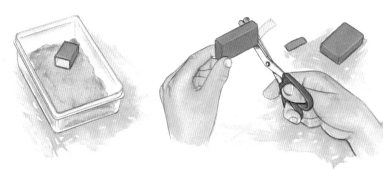

2 Cut a side out of three small cardboard boxes. Put one of these dens in each plastic box.

3 Put woodlice in one box, centipedes in the second and spiders in the third. Cover the boxes with clear film. Make several tiny holes in the clear film.

You will need: three large clear plastic boxes, damp soil, woodlice, spiders, centipedes, round-ended scissors, clear film (plastic wrap), three small cardboard boxes, cocktail stick or toothpick to make holes in the film.

Woodlice like damp, dark places. They will spend most of their time in the dark den. Centipedes live in dark places. They hunt at night. They spend more time in the dark than the light. Spiders are hunters. Some of them hide in dark places. Many spiders spend time hunting in the light.

4 Keep the animals for a day or two. Check them three or four times a day. Count the numbers in the light and dark. Keep a record of what you find. Which animal spends most time in the dark?

These children are watching how the animals behave. Remember, the animals need soil if they are kept for a few hours.

All change

All living things produce young. Some animals change
a lot as they grow up – the babies look completely
different from the adults. Others look like little adults.

Water babies

Look at this picture. Can you
see the eggs wrapped in
jelly? They are frog's eggs.
Can you see the tiny black
animals swimming
around? They are baby
frogs called **tadpoles**.
They live in water.
Soon they will grow
legs, lose their tails
and hop on to land.

▼ Kittens look a lot like adult cats.

► Adult frogs live on land and in the water. They have short bodies and no tails. They have small front legs and strong back legs for jumping.

Jump!

You will need: paper, pencils in various shades, round-ended scissors, wool, sticky tape, small metal spring.

1 Draw a large frog shape on paper (you can trace this one). Cut it out. Make another one, but this time draw on the opposite side.

3 Press the spring down and let it go. Watch your frog hop.

2 Tape a piece of wool to the back of each frog. Tie one to each side of a spring.

Butterfly babies

You can learn a lot about life cycles by keeping caterpillars.

Watch a caterpillar grow

You will need: scissors, cardboard box, strong adhesive tape, fine netting, non-hardening clay, rubber gloves, fresh leaves, kitchen paper, collecting jar, ruler, pencil, notebook, field guide, pencils or crayons in various shades.

1 Cut holes in the sides of the box for windows. Using strong tape, stick pieces of netting over the windows to cover them.

3 Wearing gloves, put fresh leaves in the cage. Make sure they are from a plant your caterpillars eat. Provide fresh leaves daily.

5 Check your caterpillars every day, replacing the leaves and damp kitchen paper. Keep a diary – how much do the caterpillars eat and how big are they?

2 Now cut a large piece of fabric to make the cage lid. Weight the corners down with clay to stop the caterpillars escaping.

4 Put some damp kitchen paper in a corner to provide moisture. Transfer your caterpillars to the box. Cover with a lid.

6 Watch how your caterpillars feed and move about. Record the dates when you see them shedding their skins. How often did they do this?

7 When it has finished growing, the caterpillar will change into a pupa, or chrysalis. It will attach itself to a twig and form a new skin. Note the date.

8 Check your pupa every day and write down the date when you see the case splitting. How long did the insect spend as a pupa?

9 You will see a butterfly or moth struggle out of the old skin. The insect rests and pumps blood into its wings to straighten them before flying.

Once the caterpillars have become adult butterflies or moths, it is time to let them go. Take the insects back to where you found them. Lift the lid off the cage and let them fly away.

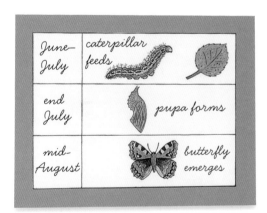

Keep a chart of the life cycles of your insects.

On the wing

Some animals, such as birds and butterflies, move by flying. They fly using wings.

▶ Look at these birds flying. What covers their bodies and wings? How do their wings move as they fly? Where are their legs and feet?

A bird's body is covered by feathers. The wings move up and down as they fly. Their legs and feet are tucked under their body out of the way.

Flutter by

Make a fluttering butterfly.
You will need: square of thin cardboard.

2 Fold up the bottom edge as shown.

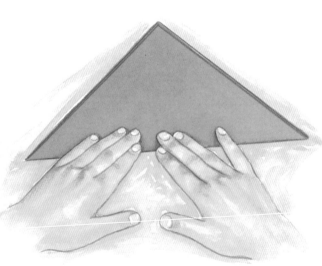

1 Take the cardboard square. Fold two corners together to make a triangle.

3 Fold the paper in half from side to side. Make sure the edges meet.

6 Pull the wings out to the side. Hold the butterfly beneath the wings. Gently throw it forwards.

Your butterfly should flutter over and over as it flies.

4 Fold back the top layer as shown.

5 Turn the paper over. Fold back the other side.

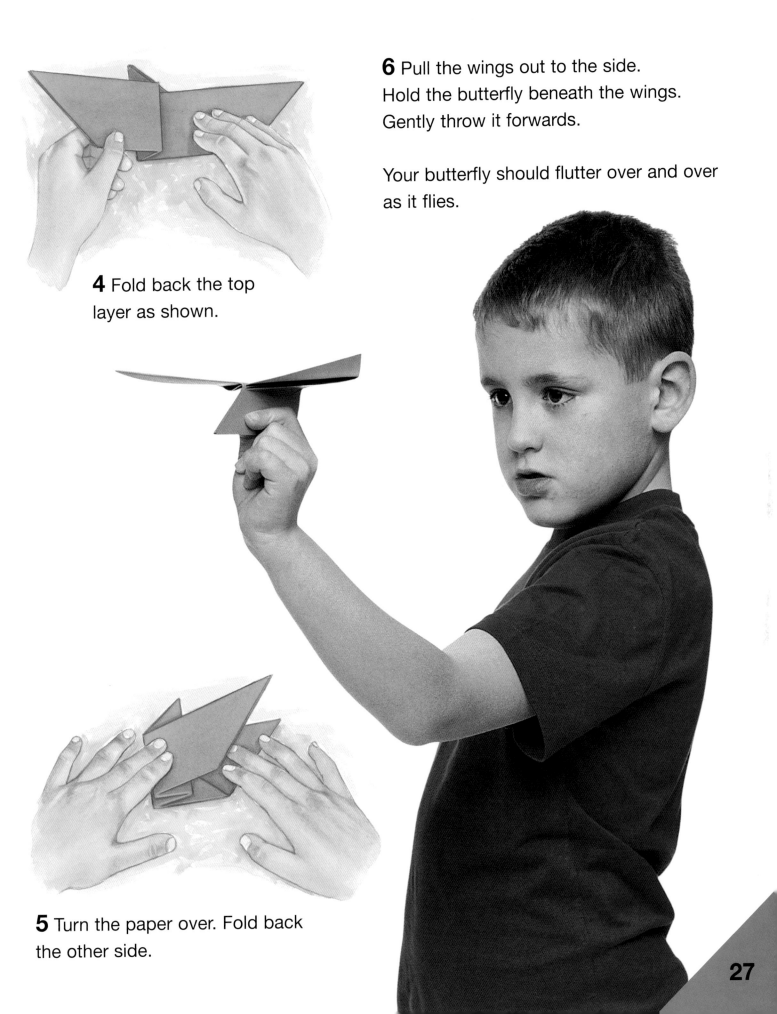

You too

Humans are animals too. People come in all shapes and sizes. What you look like will depend on your parents and where you live.

You will need: thin white cardboard, sharp pencil, pencils in various shades, round-ended scissors, paper fasteners, thin string, sticky tape, thin stick.

Move and bend

You can move and bend easily because you have joints. Try making this jointed puppet.

1 Draw and cut out body, leg and arm shapes from cardboard. Draw on the crosses as shown.

2 With a sharp pencil, make a hole in the cardboard through the crosses.

3 Use paper fasteners to join the leg pieces together. Do the same with the arms. Join the legs and arms to the body.

4 Tape some thin string to the head and hands.

5 Tie the other ends of the string to a thin stick. Make your puppet move.

28

Roller or not?

You will need: friends to help you! Look at your friends. In what ways are they the same as you? How are they different from you? Sometimes differences are hidden. Ask your friends if they can roll their tongues into a tube. How many are rollers? How many are non-rollers?

Hints to helpers

Pages 6 and 7

Talk about what makes things living or non-living, e.g. whether they can grow, move, have young, respond to what is going on around them. Ask the children to think about the main differences between plants and animals. Discuss why the apple is no longer living and what will happen to it after a while.

As the children make the rock animals, talk about what they could put on their animals to make them like real animals. Discuss what each part is used for, e.g. eyes for seeing, ears for hearing, nose for smelling, legs for moving. Compare them with the senses the children have and how they use them.

Pages 8 and 9

Talk about green plants and why animals need plants to live. Explain why it is important not to cut down too many forests. Talk about the different kinds of green plant. Look at the different parts of a flowering plant and discuss what each part is used for. Discuss the conditions plants need to grow well.

Pages 10 and 11

Discuss why some plants have flowers. Most flowers contain the male and female parts of a plant which make new plants. Explain how some flowers attract bees and other animals to land on them. The animals then spread the pollen to other flowers. Discuss other ways the pollen could be spread, e.g. by the wind. Explain why plants need to make so much pollen, e.g. some animals feed on pollen grains, and wind blows pollen around, so a lot of it is lost.

Pages 12 and 13

Talk about why plants make seeds and why the seeds need to be spread away from the parent plant. This is linked with what a plant needs to grow well. Mention that if plants are crowded together they may not get enough water and light etc. Discuss the different ways seeds can be taken from one place to another, e.g. very light seeds can be blown by the wind, sticky seeds can get stuck to the fur or feet of animals.

Pages 14 and 15

Talk about why plants make new plants and why gardeners and farmers use seeds to grow food. Discuss the different things a seed needs in order to germinate and develop into a healthy plant. Explain why farmers and gardeners need to water and feed plants to help them grow. Lead on to what happens to plants if there is a drought or if the seedlings grow in places where there is little sunlight, water or food.

Pages 16 and 17

Ask the children to think of as many different kinds of animal as they can. Talk about the different kinds of animals and compare their shapes to people's shapes. Talk about the different ways animals move and why they need to move, e.g. looking for a safe place to rest, hunting for food. Discuss what the snail uses its shell for, e.g. to protect its soft body, to stop it from drying out. Talk about what snails eat and why they have tentacles. Look at the worms and talk about why they can live in the earth and wriggle through the soil.

Talk about why we need to care for all animals, even tiny ones. Discuss where snails and worms are found and why we should always return them to the places they were found.

Pages 18 and 19

Explain that we need to take great care not to hurt small animals when picking them up. It is better to use a spoon or trowel to pick them up rather than your fingers. This will stop the animals from being damaged as well as protecting you. Explain that the children should never try to pick up a wasp or bee as they may sting, which could be dangerous.

Always collect black garden ants, not red ones as these can 'sting' and cause a rash. Ant nests can usually be found in fairly sheltered places near or under stones or plants. The entrance to the nest is often a round hole and a stream of ants is usually going in and out. The oval, cream eggs are about the size of a small grain of rice. Great care should be taken in picking up some ants and eggs. Make sure that you collect several ants for each egg. The soil will naturally contain bits of food for the ants, but you could put some bits of bread and grains of sugar on the top of the soil as extra food. Make sure the ants and eggs are returned to a suitable place when the children have watched them for a week or so.

Pages 20 and 21

Talk about why different animals live in different places, e.g. birds fly in the sky and nest in trees, worms live in the soil, etc. Discuss why some animals prefer damp, dark places and others like light, open places. Make sure that the children take great care when they collect the animals. Only keep them for a day or two at the most, then return them to the place where they were found.

Pages 22 and 23

Talk about why animals have young and the different kinds of young that various animals have. Talk about how some animals, such as frogs, change their shape and where they live as they grow up. Talk about the shape of the tadpole and how it is best suited for a life in the water. Then look at the adult frog and discuss how its big back legs and strong muscles help it to jump on land and swim through the water. Talk about how it uses its legs like a spring to push off from the ground and leap along. Discuss how the young of insects change, e.g. from caterpillars to butterflies. Link this to how people change as they grow up.

Pages 24 and 25

Explain that when butterflies and moths change during their lives, this is called complete metamorphosis. Other insects, such as ants and bees, also undergo this process. The children should look for caterpillars on plants that have half-eaten leaves and stems. Caterpillars may be found hiding on the undersides of leaves. Encourage the children to note the plant on which the caterpillars were found and take some of the leaves with them. The caterpillars of small tortoiseshell butterflies, used in this project, feed on stinging nettles. Use a field guide to

identify the species found. Check the field guide to see which plant they prefer. When picking up caterpillars, use a paintbrush, or encourage them to climb on to a leaf. It is perfectly safe to handle the majority of caterpillars from temperate regions of the world, though some have spines that might cause blisters to soft skin such as the inside of the arm. Caterpillars with hind projections, such as the horns at the tail of hawkmoth caterpillars, do not sting in any way. Carry the caterpillars home in a collecting jar. At home, keep the cage out of direct sunlight, in a moist, cool place, and try to disturb the caterpillars as little as possible.

Pages 26 and 27

Talk about the different kinds of flying animals – insects, bats and birds. Discuss the things that they have in common – wings, light bodies etc. Discuss the different ways they fly, how they use their wings and what they do with their wings when not flying.

Pages 28 and 29

Talk about the fact that people are animals too and similar in some ways to wild animals. Using the puppet, discuss how people move, talk and use their senses to help them live.

Encourage the children to think about how they are the same as their friends and in what ways they are different, e.g. size, hair, eyes, likes and dislikes in food.

31

Glossary

Anthers The parts of a flower that make pollen.

Colony A group of animals that live together.

Cones The parts of a conifer tree that contain the male or female 'cells'. Seeds grow inside the female cone.

Fruits The parts of a flowering plant that contain the seeds.

Germinate When a seed starts to grow into a new plant.

Nectar A sweet, sugary liquid made by flowers.

Nest A special place made and lived in by an animal. Some animals lay their eggs or bring up their babies in a nest.

Ovules The female 'cells' of a plant that can grow into a seed.

Petals The bright parts of a flower that attract bees.

Photosynthesis The way in which green plants make food. They make sugar from water and carbon dioxide gas using energy from sunlight.

Pollen Tiny yellow grains produced by a flower or cone. They contain the male 'cells' of the plant.

Seed The tiny part of a plant formed when female and male 'cells' join together. A seed can grow into a new plant.

Stigma Female part of a flower, which collects the pollen grains.

Tadpoles Young frogs. A tadpole has a head and a tail but no legs. The legs grow as the tadpole gets bigger.

Tentacles Long, thin finger-like parts on the bodies of animals such as snails. They are used for feeling and seeing.

Water vapour Very tiny droplets of water in the air. They are often too small for you to see.